WELCOME TO YOUR
DAILY PLANNER
LOVELY AUTHOR!

THIS PLANNER BELONGS TO:

Property of
Heather Noëlle Rhodes Johnson

COPYRIGHT AND PERMISSIONS

THE NOVEL PLANNER

A DAILY PLANNER FOR AUTHORS

Copyright © 2015 by Kristen A. Kieffer. All rights reserved.

All rights reserved. No part of this publication may be reproduced, distributed, or transmitted in any form or by any means, including photocopying, recording, or other electronic or mechanical methods, without the prior written permission of the publisher, except in the case of brief quotations embodied in critical reviews and certain other noncommercial uses permitted by copyright law.

The information provided within this book is for general informational purposes only. While we try to keep the information up-to-date and correct, there are no representations or warranties, express or implied, about the completeness, accuracy, reliability, suitability or availability with respect to the information, products, services, or related graphics contained in this book for any purpose. Any use of this information is at your own risk.

The methods described within this planner are the author's personal thoughts. They are not intended to be a definitive set of instructions for this project. You may discover there are other methods and materials to accomplish the same end result.

Requests to the author for permission should be addressed to the following email: kristen@shesnovel.com. You may also mail requests to the following address:

Kristen A Kieffer
PO Box 225
Woodstown, NJ
08098

Please feel free to take photographs of this planner (or your use of it) for the purposes of review or social media sharing. Please do not photograph the entire planner.

Printed by CreateSpace.

TABLE OF CONTENTS

WELCOME TO YOUR PLANNER	04
NOVEL PROJECT REFERENCE GUIDE	07
- PROJECT #1	
- PROJECT #2	
MONTHLY AND WEEKLY CALENDARS	21
BRAINSTORMING AND RESOURCE CENTER	169
- STORY IDEA LIST	170
- TO BE READ LIST	171
- SKETCH SPACE	172
YEARLY ACHIEVEMENT TRACKER	177

WELCOME TO YOUR PLANNER!

YOU HAVE A PASSION FOR STORIES.

But then again, you probably know that. You have this planner in your hands; you're clearly ready to tackle your next year in the wonderful world of novel-writing.

Whether you are whipping up your debut novel, looking to organize your hectic life as a full-time author, or floating somewhere in between, this is the planner for you. By outlining your upcoming projects, setting project goals, and identifying deadlines, you will be able to set daily, weekly, and monthly actionable steps that will help you knock your novel(s) out of the park.

This twelve-month planner can be used beginning in any month. Simply fill in the appropriate dates, and then conquer the world!

GET TO KNOW YOUR PLANNER

STEP ONE: First things first, on pages 06 - 19, take the time to sketch out your projects. By creating a bullet-point outline and writing down each project's genre, estimated word count, summary, character roles, settings, themes, and motifs, you will create a quick reference guide that will help you maintain consistency as you set goals and get to work.

Bonus Tip: You may want to record your references in pencil for easy erasure should your novel change with time.

STEP TWO: Don't forget to craft your character sketches. Characters are the backbone of your work; their actions form the basis of your novel's plot. Make sure that you create well-developed characters using the prompts provided in the character sketch portion of your projects' reference guides.

Want to flesh out your characters even further? Head on over to http://shesnovel.com/characters.

WELCOME TO YOUR PLANNER!

STEP THREE: It's time to plan! In the monthly and weekly calendar section of this planner, you can establish monthly, weekly, and daily goals for your work and track your accomplishments as you make them. You can also craft weekly work, personal, and project to-do lists, sketch out any new ideas you have brainstormed, set reminders for deadlines and events, and track your word count progress.

Bonus Tip: Each month contains five weekly spreads. You may or may not need all five weeks, depending on the month.

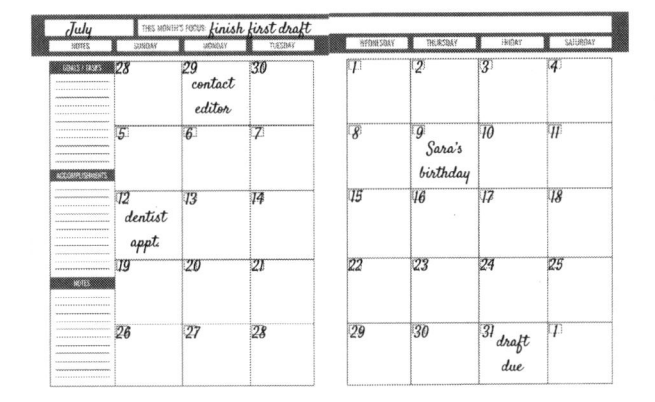

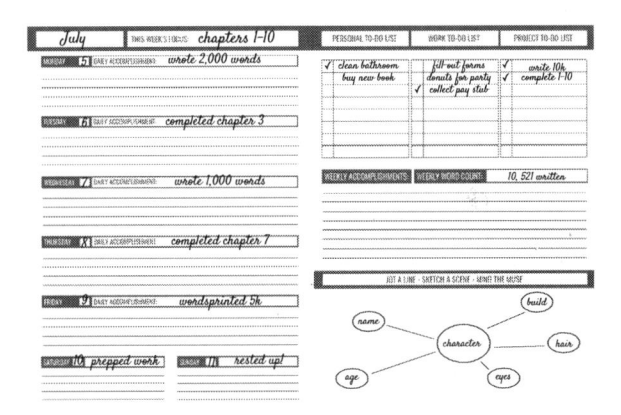

Don't forget to check out the quotes from industry professionals at the bottom of each page for instant inspiration.

STEP FOUR: Have fun and stay organized using the lists provided in the brainstorming and resources center on pages 168 - 175. Record all of your story ideas, organize your to-be-read list, and write out or doodle all of your brainstorms and daydreams.

STEP FIVE: Using the space on pages 178 -179, track your accomplishments throughout the year. Doing so will help you see just how far you have come, as well as where you might head in your next year of novel planning.

STEP SIX: Your novel won't write itself! Now is the time to brew yourself a nice cup of caffeine, free the muse, and get to work. Continue to refer back to and adjust your project reference guides and achievements tracker as necessary throughout the year. Enjoy!

> "A PROFESSIONAL WRITER IS AN AMATEUR WHO DIDN'T QUIT."

—RICHARD BACH, BEST-SELLING AUTHOR

CHARACTER SKETCH

NAME: _____ **ROLE:** _____

APPEARANCE:

AGE: _____ ETHNICITY: _____
BUILD: _____
NOTABLE FEATURES: _____
_____
_____
_____

BACKSTORY:

_____
_____
_____
_____
_____
_____

PERSONALITY:

STRENGTHS: _____
_____
FLAWS: _____
_____
GOALS: _____
_____
MOTIVATIONS: _____
_____
_____

STORY ARC:

_____
_____
_____
_____
_____
_____
_____
_____

NAME: _____ **ROLE:** _____

APPEARANCE:

AGE: _____ ETHNICITY: _____
BUILD: _____
NOTABLE FEATURES: _____
_____
_____
_____

BACKSTORY:

_____
_____
_____
_____
_____
_____

PERSONALITY:

STRENGTHS: _____
_____
FLAWS: _____
_____
GOALS: _____
_____
MOTIVATIONS: _____
_____
_____

STORY ARC:

_____
_____
_____
_____
_____
_____
_____
_____

CHARACTER SKETCH

NAME: **ROLE:**

APPEARANCE:

AGE: _____ ETHNICITY: _____
BUILD: _____
NOTABLE FEATURES: _____
_____
_____
_____

BACKSTORY:

_____
_____
_____
_____
_____
_____

PERSONALITY:

STRENGTHS: _____
_____
FLAWS: _____
_____
GOALS: _____
_____
MOTIVATIONS: _____
_____
_____

STORY ARC:

_____
_____
_____
_____
_____
_____
_____
_____
_____

NAME: **ROLE:**

APPEARANCE:

AGE: _____ ETHNICITY: _____
BUILD: _____
NOTABLE FEATURES: _____
_____
_____
_____

BACKSTORY:

_____
_____
_____
_____
_____
_____

PERSONALITY:

STRENGTHS: _____
_____
FLAWS: _____
_____
GOALS: _____
_____
MOTIVATIONS: _____
_____
_____

STORY ARC:

_____
_____
_____
_____
_____
_____
_____
_____
_____

CHARACTER SKETCH

NAME: _____   ROLE: _____

APPEARANCE:

AGE: _____ ETHNICITY: _____
BUILD: _____
NOTABLE FEATURES: _____
_____
_____
_____

PERSONALITY:

STRENGTHS: _____
_____
FLAWS: _____
_____
GOALS: _____
_____
MOTIVATIONS: _____
_____
_____

BACKSTORY:

_____
_____
_____
_____
_____
_____

STORY ARC:

_____
_____
_____
_____
_____
_____
_____
_____
_____

NAME: _____   ROLE: _____

APPEARANCE:

AGE: _____ ETHNICITY: _____
BUILD: _____
NOTABLE FEATURES: _____
_____
_____
_____

PERSONALITY:

STRENGTHS: _____
_____
FLAWS: _____
_____
GOALS: _____
_____
MOTIVATIONS: _____
_____
_____

BACKSTORY:

_____
_____
_____
_____
_____
_____

STORY ARC:

_____
_____
_____
_____
_____
_____
_____
_____
_____

PROJECT GOALS

✓	DEADLINE	GOAL	REWARD

PROJECT MARKETING STRATEGY

Where will you market your book once it is published?

- [ ] FACEBOOK
- [ ] TWITTER
- [ ] GOOGLE+
- [ ] INSTAGRAM
- [ ] PINTEREST
- [ ] YOUTUBE
- [ ] GOODREADS
- [ ] BLOG POSTS
- [ ] ONLINE FORUMS
- [ ] BOOK SIGNINGS
- [ ] BOOK TOURS
- [ ] WRITING CONFERENCES
- [ ]
- [ ]
- [ ]
- [ ]
- [ ]

Choose your top four marketing steams (listed to the left), and write a brief marketing strategy for each.

MARKETING STREAM: _____
_____
_____
_____
_____
_____

MARKETING STREAM: _____
_____
_____
_____
_____
_____

MARKETING STREAM: _____
_____
_____
_____
_____
_____

MARKETING STREAM: _____
_____
_____
_____
_____
_____

"WITHOUT LEAPS OF IMAGINATION, OR DREAMING, WE LOSE THE EXCITEMENT OF POSSIBILITIES. DREAMING, AFTER ALL, IS A FORM OF PLANNING."

-GLORIA STEINEM, JOURNALIST AND POLITICAL ACTIVIST

WELCOME TO YOUR MONTHLY & WEEKLY CALENDARS

PLAN YOUR PATH TO PASSION PROJECT SUCCESS.

~~September, 2016~~ February, 2017

THIS MONTH'S FOCUS: Outlining, plotting,

NOTES	SUNDAY	MONDAY	TUESDAY
GOALS / TASKS Determine point of book Develop outline	☐	☐	☐
	4	5 WRITE	6
ACCOMPLISHMENTS	11	12	13
	18 Sub-plot focus	19	20
NOTES	25	26	27

22   "A better way to write complex characters is, ironically, to simplify them." -Dana Bate

STARTING

WEDNESDAY	THURSDAY	FRIDAY	SATURDAY
	1	2	3
7	8	9	10
14	15	16 Start plotting	17 Start writing
21	22	23	24
28	~~29~~	~~30~~	

"I write to give myself strength. I write to be the characters I am not." -Joss Whedon

Sept 12 ~~$8~~ February 5-11

THIS WEEK'S FOCUS: Starting

MONDAY | 5 | DAILY ACCOMPLISHMENT:

TUESDAY | 6 | DAILY ACCOMPLISHMENT:

WEDNESDAY | 7 | DAILY ACCOMPLISHMENT:

THURSDAY | 8 | DAILY ACCOMPLISHMENT:

FRIDAY | ✓ | DAILY ACCOMPLISHMENT: ~~Started outlining~~ organizing
~~Print sheets~~
~~Brainstorm~~

SATURDAY | | ~~Start outlining~~
~~Brainstorm more~~
~~Put together ideas~~
~~Start writing~~

SUNDAY | | ~~Fleshout sub-plots~~
~~Write 1000 words~~

PERSONAL TO-DO LIST	WORK TO-DO LIST	PROJECT TO-DO LIST
Finish school stuff		Have something coherent written. Outline and figure out what the actual plot is

WEEKLY ACCOMPLISHMENTS: **WEEKLY WORD COUNT:**

_____
_____
_____
_____
_____
_____
_____
_____

JOT A LINE - SKETCH A SCENE - MIND THE MUSE

"There is no greater agony than bearing an untold story inside you." -Maya Angelou

THIS WEEK'S FOCUS:

MONDAY   DAILY ACCOMPLISHMENT:

_____
_____
_____
_____

TUESDAY   DAILY ACCOMPLISHMENT:

_____
_____
_____
_____

WEDNESDAY   DAILY ACCOMPLISHMENT:

_____
_____
_____
_____

THURSDAY   DAILY ACCOMPLISHMENT:

_____
_____
_____
_____

FRIDAY   DAILY ACCOMPLISHMENT:

_____
_____
_____
_____

SATURDAY	**SUNDAY**
_____	_____
_____	_____
_____	_____

PERSONAL TO-DO LIST	WORK TO-DO LIST	PROJECT TO-DO LIST

WEEKLY ACCOMPLISHMENTS: **WEEKLY WORD COUNT:**

JOT A LINE - SKETCH A SCENE - MIND THE MUSE

"If you don't have time to read, you don't have the time (or the tools) to write. Simple as that." -Stephen King

THIS WEEK'S FOCUS:

MONDAY DAILY ACCOMPLISHMENT:

_____
_____
_____

TUESDAY DAILY ACCOMPLISHMENT:

_____
_____
_____

WEDNESDAY DAILY ACCOMPLISHMENT:

_____
_____
_____

THURSDAY DAILY ACCOMPLISHMENT:

_____
_____
_____

FRIDAY DAILY ACCOMPLISHMENT:

_____
_____
_____

SATURDAY	**SUNDAY**
_____	_____
_____	_____
_____	_____

PERSONAL TO-DO LIST	WORK TO-DO LIST	PROJECT TO-DO LIST

WEEKLY ACCOMPLISHMENTS: **WEEKLY WORD COUNT:**

JOT A LINE - SKETCH A SCENE - MIND THE MUSE

"You can't wait for inspiration. You have to go after it with a club." -Jack London

THIS WEEK'S FOCUS:

MONDAY | **DAILY ACCOMPLISHMENT:**

_____
_____
_____

TUESDAY | **DAILY ACCOMPLISHMENT:**

_____
_____
_____

WEDNESDAY | **DAILY ACCOMPLISHMENT:**

_____
_____
_____

THURSDAY | **DAILY ACCOMPLISHMENT:**

_____
_____
_____

FRIDAY | **DAILY ACCOMPLISHMENT:**

_____
_____
_____

SATURDAY

_____
_____
_____

SUNDAY

_____
_____
_____

PERSONAL TO-DO LIST	WORK TO-DO LIST	PROJECT TO-DO LIST

WEEKLY ACCOMPLISHMENTS: **WEEKLY WORD COUNT:**

JOT A LINE - SKETCH A SCENE - MIND THE MUSE

"Always be a poet, even in prose." -Charles Baudelaire

THIS WEEK'S FOCUS:

MONDAY   DAILY ACCOMPLISHMENT:
_____
_____
_____

TUESDAY   DAILY ACCOMPLISHMENT:
_____
_____
_____

WEDNESDAY   DAILY ACCOMPLISHMENT:
_____
_____
_____

THURSDAY   DAILY ACCOMPLISHMENT:
_____
_____
_____

FRIDAY   DAILY ACCOMPLISHMENT:
_____
_____
_____

SATURDAY	**SUNDAY**
_____	_____
_____	_____
_____	_____

PERSONAL TO-DO LIST	WORK TO-DO LIST	PROJECT TO-DO LIST

WEEKLY ACCOMPLISHMENTS: **WEEKLY WORD COUNT:**

JOT A LINE - SKETCH A SCENE - MIND THE MUSE

"Tears are words that need to be written." -Paulo Coehlo

THIS MONTH'S FOCUS:

NOTES	SUNDAY	MONDAY	TUESDAY

GOALS / TASKS

ACCOMPLISHMENTS

NOTES

"If you don't see the book you want on the shelf, write it." -Beverly Cleary

WEDNESDAY	THURSDAY	FRIDAY	SATURDAY

"Very few writers really know what they are doing until they've done it." -Anne Lamott

THIS WEEK'S FOCUS:

MONDAY ☐ DAILY ACCOMPLISHMENT:

___
___
___

TUESDAY ☐ DAILY ACCOMPLISHMENT:

___
___
___

WEDNESDAY ☐ DAILY ACCOMPLISHMENT:

___
___
___

THURSDAY ☐ DAILY ACCOMPLISHMENT:

___
___
___

FRIDAY ☐ DAILY ACCOMPLISHMENT:

___
___
___

SATURDAY ☐   **SUNDAY** ☐

___
___
___

PERSONAL TO-DO LIST	WORK TO-DO LIST	PROJECT TO-DO LIST

WEEKLY ACCOMPLISHMENTS: **WEEKLY WORD COUNT:**

JOT A LINE - SKETCH A SCENE - MIND THE MUSE

"Amateurs sit and wait for inspiration, the rest of us just get up and go to work." -Stephen King

THIS WEEK'S FOCUS:

MONDAY ☐ DAILY ACCOMPLISHMENT:
_____
_____
_____

TUESDAY ☐ DAILY ACCOMPLISHMENT:
_____
_____
_____

WEDNESDAY ☐ DAILY ACCOMPLISHMENT:
_____
_____
_____

THURSDAY ☐ DAILY ACCOMPLISHMENT:
_____
_____
_____

FRIDAY ☐ DAILY ACCOMPLISHMENT:
_____
_____
_____

SATURDAY ☐   **SUNDAY** ☐
_____   _____
_____   _____
_____   _____

PERSONAL TO-DO LIST	WORK TO-DO LIST	PROJECT TO-DO LIST

WEEKLY ACCOMPLISHMENTS: **WEEKLY WORD COUNT:**

JOT A LINE - SKETCH A SCENE - MIND THE MUSE

"Take chances. It may be bad, but it's the only way you can do anything really good." -William Faulkner

THIS WEEK'S FOCUS:

MONDAY　　DAILY ACCOMPLISHMENT:

_____
_____
_____

TUESDAY 　DAILY ACCOMPLISHMENT:

_____
_____
_____

WEDNESDAY 　DAILY ACCOMPLISHMENT:

_____
_____
_____

THURSDAY 　DAILY ACCOMPLISHMENT:

_____
_____
_____

FRIDAY 　DAILY ACCOMPLISHMENT:

_____
_____
_____

SATURDAY　　　　　　　　　　　　　　**SUNDAY**

_____　　　_____
_____　　　_____
_____　　　_____

PERSONAL TO-DO LIST	WORK TO-DO LIST	PROJECT TO-DO LIST

WEEKLY ACCOMPLISHMENTS: **WEEKLY WORD COUNT:**

JOT A LINE - SKETCH A SCENE - MIND THE MUSE

"A word after a word after a word is power." -Margaret Atwood

THIS WEEK'S FOCUS:

MONDAY ☐ DAILY ACCOMPLISHMENT:

_____
_____
_____

TUESDAY ☐ DAILY ACCOMPLISHMENT:

_____
_____
_____

WEDNESDAY ☐ DAILY ACCOMPLISHMENT:

_____
_____
_____

THURSDAY ☐ DAILY ACCOMPLISHMENT:

_____
_____
_____

FRIDAY ☐ DAILY ACCOMPLISHMENT:

_____
_____
_____

SATURDAY ☐	**SUNDAY** ☐
_____	_____
_____	_____
_____	_____

PERSONAL TO-DO LIST	WORK TO-DO LIST	PROJECT TO-DO LIST

WEEKLY ACCOMPLISHMENTS: **WEEKLY WORD COUNT:**

JOT A LINE - SKETCH A SCENE - MIND THE MUSE

"You can make anything by writing." -C.S. Lewis

THIS WEEK'S FOCUS:

MONDAY DAILY ACCOMPLISHMENT:

TUESDAY DAILY ACCOMPLISHMENT:

WEDNESDAY DAILY ACCOMPLISHMENT:

THURSDAY DAILY ACCOMPLISHMENT:

FRIDAY DAILY ACCOMPLISHMENT:

SATURDAY   **SUNDAY**

PERSONAL TO-DO LIST	WORK TO-DO LIST	PROJECT TO-DO LIST

WEEKLY ACCOMPLISHMENTS: **WEEKLY WORD COUNT:**

JOT A LINE - SKETCH A SCENE - MIND THE MUSE

"Imagination is like a muscle. I found out that the more I wrote, the bigger it got." -Philip Jose Farmer

THIS MONTH'S FOCUS:

NOTES	SUNDAY	MONDAY	TUESDAY

GOALS / TASKS

ACCOMPLISHMENTS

NOTES

"A book is a dream that you hold in your hand." -Neil Gaiman

WEDNESDAY	THURSDAY	FRIDAY	SATURDAY

"As a writer, you ask yourself to dream while awake." -Aimee Bender

THIS WEEK'S FOCUS:

MONDAY   DAILY ACCOMPLISHMENT:
_____
_____
_____

TUESDAY   DAILY ACCOMPLISHMENT:
_____
_____
_____

WEDNESDAY   DAILY ACCOMPLISHMENT:
_____
_____
_____

THURSDAY   DAILY ACCOMPLISHMENT:
_____
_____
_____

FRIDAY   DAILY ACCOMPLISHMENT:
_____
_____
_____

SATURDAY   **SUNDAY**
_____   _____
_____   _____
_____   _____

PERSONAL TO-DO LIST	WORK TO-DO LIST	PROJECT TO-DO LIST

WEEKLY ACCOMPLISHMENTS: **WEEKLY WORD COUNT:**

JOT A LINE - SKETCH A SCENE - MIND THE MUSE

"I write to explore all the things I'm afraid of." -Joss Whedon

THIS WEEK'S FOCUS:

MONDAY DAILY ACCOMPLISHMENT:

TUESDAY DAILY ACCOMPLISHMENT:

WEDNESDAY DAILY ACCOMPLISHMENT:

THURSDAY DAILY ACCOMPLISHMENT:

FRIDAY DAILY ACCOMPLISHMENT:

SATURDAY　　　　　　　　　　　　　**SUNDAY**

PERSONAL TO-DO LIST	WORK TO-DO LIST	PROJECT TO-DO LIST

WEEKLY ACCOMPLISHMENTS: **WEEKLY WORD COUNT:**

JOT A LINE - SKETCH A SCENE - MIND THE MUSE

"There is nothing to writing. All you do is sit down at a typewriter and bleed." -Ernest Hemingway

THIS WEEK'S FOCUS:

MONDAY DAILY ACCOMPLISHMENT:

TUESDAY DAILY ACCOMPLISHMENT:

WEDNESDAY DAILY ACCOMPLISHMENT:

THURSDAY DAILY ACCOMPLISHMENT:

FRIDAY DAILY ACCOMPLISHMENT:

SATURDAY

SUNDAY

PERSONAL TO-DO LIST	WORK TO-DO LIST	PROJECT TO-DO LIST

WEEKLY ACCOMPLISHMENTS: **WEEKLY WORD COUNT:**

JOT A LINE - SKETCH A SCENE - MIND THE MUSE

"Let me live, love, and say it well in good sentences." -Sylvia Plath

THIS WEEK'S FOCUS:

MONDAY ☐ DAILY ACCOMPLISHMENT:

TUESDAY ☐ DAILY ACCOMPLISHMENT:

WEDNESDAY ☐ DAILY ACCOMPLISHMENT:

THURSDAY ☐ DAILY ACCOMPLISHMENT:

FRIDAY ☐ DAILY ACCOMPLISHMENT:

SATURDAY ☐

SUNDAY ☐

PERSONAL TO-DO LIST	WORK TO-DO LIST	PROJECT TO-DO LIST

WEEKLY ACCOMPLISHMENTS: **WEEKLY WORD COUNT:**

JOT A LINE - SKETCH A SCENE - MIND THE MUSE

"Today was a good writing day, and on the good writing days nothing else matters." -Neil Gaiman

THIS WEEK'S FOCUS:

MONDAY DAILY ACCOMPLISHMENT:

TUESDAY DAILY ACCOMPLISHMENT:

WEDNESDAY DAILY ACCOMPLISHMENT:

THURSDAY DAILY ACCOMPLISHMENT:

FRIDAY DAILY ACCOMPLISHMENT:

SATURDAY

SUNDAY

PERSONAL TO-DO LIST	WORK TO-DO LIST	PROJECT TO-DO LIST

WEEKLY ACCOMPLISHMENTS: **WEEKLY WORD COUNT:**

JOT A LINE - SKETCH A SCENE - MIND THE MUSE

"There are three rules for writing a novel. Unfortunately, no one knows what they are." -W. Somerset Maugham

THIS MONTH'S FOCUS:

NOTES	SUNDAY	MONDAY	TUESDAY

GOALS / TASKS

ACCOMPLISHMENTS

NOTES

"You need a certain amount of nerve to be a writer." -Margaret Atwood

WEDNESDAY	THURSDAY	FRIDAY	SATURDAY

"Almost all good writing begins with terrible first efforts. You need to start somewhere." -Anne Lamott

THIS WEEK'S FOCUS:

MONDAY ☐ DAILY ACCOMPLISHMENT:
_____
_____
_____

TUESDAY ☐ DAILY ACCOMPLISHMENT:
_____
_____
_____

WEDNESDAY ☐ DAILY ACCOMPLISHMENT:
_____
_____
_____

THURSDAY ☐ DAILY ACCOMPLISHMENT:
_____
_____
_____

FRIDAY ☐ DAILY ACCOMPLISHMENT:
_____
_____
_____

SATURDAY ☐   **SUNDAY** ☐
_____   _____
_____   _____
_____   _____

PERSONAL TO-DO LIST	WORK TO-DO LIST	PROJECT TO-DO LIST

WEEKLY ACCOMPLISHMENTS: **WEEKLY WORD COUNT:**

JOT A LINE - SKETCH A SCENE - MIND THE MUSE

"When writing a novel a writer should create living people; people not characters." -Ernest Hemingway

THIS WEEK'S FOCUS:

MONDAY ☐ DAILY ACCOMPLISHMENT:
_____
_____
_____

TUESDAY ☐ DAILY ACCOMPLISHMENT:
_____
_____
_____

WEDNESDAY ☐ DAILY ACCOMPLISHMENT:
_____
_____
_____

THURSDAY ☐ DAILY ACCOMPLISHMENT:
_____
_____
_____

FRIDAY ☐ DAILY ACCOMPLISHMENT:
_____
_____
_____

SATURDAY ☐ _____   **SUNDAY** ☐ _____
_____   _____
_____   _____
_____   _____

PERSONAL TO-DO LIST	WORK TO-DO LIST	PROJECT TO-DO LIST

WEEKLY ACCOMPLISHMENTS: **WEEKLY WORD COUNT:**

JOT A LINE - SKETCH A SCENE - MIND THE MUSE

"Either write something worth reading, or do something worth writing." -Benjamin Franklin

THIS WEEK'S FOCUS:

MONDAY DAILY ACCOMPLISHMENT:

TUESDAY DAILY ACCOMPLISHMENT:

WEDNESDAY DAILY ACCOMPLISHMENT:

THURSDAY DAILY ACCOMPLISHMENT:

FRIDAY DAILY ACCOMPLISHMENT:

SATURDAY

SUNDAY

PERSONAL TO-DO LIST	WORK TO-DO LIST	PROJECT TO-DO LIST

WEEKLY ACCOMPLISHMENTS: **WEEKLY WORD COUNT:**

JOT A LINE - SKETCH A SCENE - MIND THE MUSE

"I can shake off everything as I write; my sorrows disappear, my courage is reborn." -Anne Frank

THIS WEEK'S FOCUS:

MONDAY ☐ DAILY ACCOMPLISHMENT:

_____
_____
_____

TUESDAY ☐ DAILY ACCOMPLISHMENT:

_____
_____
_____

WEDNESDAY ☐ DAILY ACCOMPLISHMENT:

_____
_____
_____

THURSDAY ☐ DAILY ACCOMPLISHMENT:

_____
_____
_____

FRIDAY ☐ DAILY ACCOMPLISHMENT:

_____
_____
_____

SATURDAY ☐   **SUNDAY** ☐

_____
_____
_____

PERSONAL TO-DO LIST	WORK TO-DO LIST	PROJECT TO-DO LIST

WEEKLY ACCOMPLISHMENTS: **WEEKLY WORD COUNT:**

_____
_____
_____
_____
_____
_____
_____
_____

JOT A LINE - SKETCH A SCENE - MIND THE MUSE

"We have to continually be jumping off cliffs and developing our wings on the way down." -Kurt Vonnegut

THIS WEEK'S FOCUS:

MONDAY DAILY ACCOMPLISHMENT:

TUESDAY DAILY ACCOMPLISHMENT:

WEDNESDAY DAILY ACCOMPLISHMENT:

THURSDAY DAILY ACCOMPLISHMENT:

FRIDAY DAILY ACCOMPLISHMENT:

SATURDAY

SUNDAY

PERSONAL TO-DO LIST	WORK TO-DO LIST	PROJECT TO-DO LIST

WEEKLY ACCOMPLISHMENTS: **WEEKLY WORD COUNT:**

JOT A LINE - SKETCH A SCENE - MIND THE MUSE

"How vain it is to sit down to write when you have not stood up to live." -Henry David Thoreau

THIS MONTH'S FOCUS:

NOTES	SUNDAY	MONDAY	TUESDAY

GOALS / TASKS

ACCOMPLISHMENTS

NOTES

"It is okay to write perfect garbage - as long as you edit brilliantly." -C.J. Cherryh

WEDNESDAY	THURSDAY	FRIDAY	SATURDAY

"Write down who you were, who you are, and what you want to remember." -Natalie Goldberg

THIS WEEK'S FOCUS:

MONDAY ☐ DAILY ACCOMPLISHMENT:

_____
_____
_____

TUESDAY ☐ DAILY ACCOMPLISHMENT:

_____
_____
_____

WEDNESDAY ☐ DAILY ACCOMPLISHMENT:

_____
_____
_____

THURSDAY ☐ DAILY ACCOMPLISHMENT:

_____
_____
_____

FRIDAY ☐ DAILY ACCOMPLISHMENT:

_____
_____
_____

SATURDAY ☐   **SUNDAY** ☐

_____   _____
_____   _____
_____   _____

PERSONAL TO-DO LIST	WORK TO-DO LIST	PROJECT TO-DO LIST

WEEKLY ACCOMPLISHMENTS: **WEEKLY WORD COUNT:**

JOT A LINE - SKETCH A SCENE - MIND THE MUSE

"You take people, you put them on a journey, you give them peril, you find out who they really are." -Joss Whedon

THIS WEEK'S FOCUS:

MONDAY ☐ DAILY ACCOMPLISHMENT:
_____
_____
_____

TUESDAY ☐ DAILY ACCOMPLISHMENT:
_____
_____
_____

WEDNESDAY ☐ DAILY ACCOMPLISHMENT:
_____
_____
_____

THURSDAY ☐ DAILY ACCOMPLISHMENT:
_____
_____
_____

FRIDAY ☐ DAILY ACCOMPLISHMENT:
_____
_____
_____

SATURDAY ☐ _____   **SUNDAY** ☐ _____
_____   _____
_____   _____
_____   _____

PERSONAL TO-DO LIST	WORK TO-DO LIST	PROJECT TO-DO LIST

WEEKLY ACCOMPLISHMENTS: **WEEKLY WORD COUNT:**

JOT A LINE - SKETCH A SCENE - MIND THE MUSE

"When we write, we start in the middle and fight our way out." -Vickie Karp

THIS WEEK'S FOCUS:

MONDAY DAILY ACCOMPLISHMENT:

TUESDAY DAILY ACCOMPLISHMENT:

WEDNESDAY DAILY ACCOMPLISHMENT:

THURSDAY DAILY ACCOMPLISHMENT:

FRIDAY DAILY ACCOMPLISHMENT:

SATURDAY

SUNDAY

PERSONAL TO-DO LIST	WORK TO-DO LIST	PROJECT TO-DO LIST

WEEKLY ACCOMPLISHMENTS: **WEEKLY WORD COUNT:**

JOT A LINE - SKETCH A SCENE - MIND THE MUSE

"After nourishment, shelter and companionship, stories are the thing we need most in the world." -Phillip Pullman

THIS WEEK'S FOCUS:

MONDAY ☐ DAILY ACCOMPLISHMENT:

_____
_____
_____

TUESDAY ☐ DAILY ACCOMPLISHMENT:

_____
_____
_____

WEDNESDAY ☐ DAILY ACCOMPLISHMENT:

_____
_____
_____

THURSDAY ☐ DAILY ACCOMPLISHMENT:

_____
_____
_____

FRIDAY ☐ DAILY ACCOMPLISHMENT:

_____
_____
_____

SATURDAY ☐   **SUNDAY** ☐

_____   _____
_____   _____
_____   _____

PERSONAL TO-DO LIST	WORK TO-DO LIST	PROJECT TO-DO LIST

WEEKLY ACCOMPLISHMENTS: **WEEKLY WORD COUNT:**

JOT A LINE - SKETCH A SCENE - MIND THE MUSE

"Don't tell me the moon is shining; show me the glint of light on broken glass." -Anton Chekhov

THIS WEEK'S FOCUS:

MONDAY ☐ DAILY ACCOMPLISHMENT:
_____
_____
_____

TUESDAY ☐ DAILY ACCOMPLISHMENT:
_____
_____
_____

WEDNESDAY ☐ DAILY ACCOMPLISHMENT:
_____
_____
_____

THURSDAY ☐ DAILY ACCOMPLISHMENT:
_____
_____
_____

FRIDAY ☐ DAILY ACCOMPLISHMENT:
_____
_____
_____

SATURDAY ☐ _____   **SUNDAY** ☐ _____
_____
_____
_____

PERSONAL TO-DO LIST	WORK TO-DO LIST	PROJECT TO-DO LIST

WEEKLY ACCOMPLISHMENTS: **WEEKLY WORD COUNT:**

JOT A LINE - SKETCH A SCENE - MIND THE MUSE

"Fiction is the truth inside the lie." -Stephen King

THIS MONTH'S FOCUS:

NOTES	SUNDAY	MONDAY	TUESDAY

GOALS / TASKS

ACCOMPLISHMENTS

NOTES

"Quantity produces quality. If you only write a few things, you're doomed." -Ray Bradbury

WEDNESDAY	THURSDAY	FRIDAY	SATURDAY

"You must learn to be three people at once: writer, character, and reader." -Nancy Kress

THIS WEEK'S FOCUS:

MONDAY ☐ DAILY ACCOMPLISHMENT:

_____
_____
_____

TUESDAY ☐ DAILY ACCOMPLISHMENT:

_____
_____
_____

WEDNESDAY ☐ DAILY ACCOMPLISHMENT:

_____
_____
_____

THURSDAY ☐ DAILY ACCOMPLISHMENT:

_____
_____
_____

FRIDAY ☐ DAILY ACCOMPLISHMENT:

_____
_____
_____

SATURDAY ☐ | **SUNDAY** ☐

_____ | _____
_____ | _____
_____ | _____

PERSONAL TO-DO LIST	WORK TO-DO LIST	PROJECT TO-DO LIST

WEEKLY ACCOMPLISHMENTS: **WEEKLY WORD COUNT:**

JOT A LINE - SKETCH A SCENE - MIND THE MUSE

"A good novel tells us the truth about its hero; but a bad novel tells us the truth about its author." -G.K. Chesterton

THIS WEEK'S FOCUS:

MONDAY ☐ DAILY ACCOMPLISHMENT:
_____
_____
_____

TUESDAY ☐ DAILY ACCOMPLISHMENT:
_____
_____
_____

WEDNESDAY ☐ DAILY ACCOMPLISHMENT:
_____
_____
_____

THURSDAY ☐ DAILY ACCOMPLISHMENT:
_____
_____
_____

FRIDAY ☐ DAILY ACCOMPLISHMENT:
_____
_____
_____

SATURDAY ☐
_____
_____
_____

SUNDAY ☐
_____
_____
_____

PERSONAL TO-DO LIST	WORK TO-DO LIST	PROJECT TO-DO LIST

WEEKLY ACCOMPLISHMENTS: **WEEKLY WORD COUNT:**

JOT A LINE - SKETCH A SCENE - MIND THE MUSE

"You can't blame a writer for what the characters say." -Truman Capote

THIS WEEK'S FOCUS:

MONDAY ☐ DAILY ACCOMPLISHMENT:

___
___
___

TUESDAY ☐ DAILY ACCOMPLISHMENT:

___
___
___

WEDNESDAY ☐ DAILY ACCOMPLISHMENT:

___
___
___

THURSDAY ☐ DAILY ACCOMPLISHMENT:

___
___
___

FRIDAY ☐ DAILY ACCOMPLISHMENT:

___
___
___

SATURDAY ☐   **SUNDAY** ☐

___
___
___

PERSONAL TO-DO LIST	WORK TO-DO LIST	PROJECT TO-DO LIST

WEEKLY ACCOMPLISHMENTS: **WEEKLY WORD COUNT:**

JOT A LINE - SKETCH A SCENE - MIND THE MUSE

"Read, read, read. Read everything - trash, classics, good and bad, and see how they do it." -William Faulkner

THIS WEEK'S FOCUS:

MONDAY   DAILY ACCOMPLISHMENT:

___

TUESDAY   DAILY ACCOMPLISHMENT:

___

WEDNESDAY   DAILY ACCOMPLISHMENT:

___

THURSDAY   DAILY ACCOMPLISHMENT:

___

FRIDAY   DAILY ACCOMPLISHMENT:

___

SATURDAY   **SUNDAY**

PERSONAL TO-DO LIST	WORK TO-DO LIST	PROJECT TO-DO LIST

WEEKLY ACCOMPLISHMENTS: **WEEKLY WORD COUNT:**

JOT A LINE - SKETCH A SCENE - MIND THE MUSE

"No tears in the writer, no tears in the reader. No surprise in the writer, no surprise in the reader." -Robert Frost

THIS WEEK'S FOCUS:

MONDAY — DAILY ACCOMPLISHMENT:
___
___
___

TUESDAY — DAILY ACCOMPLISHMENT:
___
___
___

WEDNESDAY — DAILY ACCOMPLISHMENT:
___
___
___

THURSDAY — DAILY ACCOMPLISHMENT:
___
___
___

FRIDAY — DAILY ACCOMPLISHMENT:
___
___
___

SATURDAY
___
___
___

SUNDAY
___
___
___

PERSONAL TO-DO LIST	WORK TO-DO LIST	PROJECT TO-DO LIST

WEEKLY ACCOMPLISHMENTS: **WEEKLY WORD COUNT:**

_____
_____
_____
_____
_____
_____
_____
_____

JOT A LINE - SKETCH A SCENE - MIND THE MUSE

"Fantasy is hardly an escape from reality. It's a way of understanding it." -Lloyd Alexander

CONGRATULATIONS, WRITER - YOU'VE BEEN NOVEL PLANNING FOR HALF A YEAR!

DON'T FORGET TO RECORD YOUR GOALS IN THE ACHIEVEMENTS TRACKER!

FIND THIS SECTION ON PAGES 176-179.

THIS MONTH'S FOCUS:

| NOTES | SUNDAY | MONDAY | TUESDAY |

GOALS / TASKS

ACCOMPLISHMENTS

NOTES

"Start writing, no matter what. The water does not flow until the faucet is turned on." -Louis L'amour

WEDNESDAY	THURSDAY	FRIDAY	SATURDAY

"One must be a little crazy to write a good novel." -John Gardner

THIS WEEK'S FOCUS:

MONDAY DAILY ACCOMPLISHMENT:

TUESDAY DAILY ACCOMPLISHMENT:

WEDNESDAY DAILY ACCOMPLISHMENT:

THURSDAY DAILY ACCOMPLISHMENT:

FRIDAY DAILY ACCOMPLISHMENT:

SATURDAY

SUNDAY

PERSONAL TO-DO LIST	WORK TO-DO LIST	PROJECT TO-DO LIST

WEEKLY ACCOMPLISHMENTS: **WEEKLY WORD COUNT:**

JOT A LINE - SKETCH A SCENE - MIND THE MUSE

"Don't be satisfied with stories, how things have gone with others. Write your own myth." -Rumi

THIS WEEK'S FOCUS:

MONDAY DAILY ACCOMPLISHMENT:

TUESDAY DAILY ACCOMPLISHMENT:

WEDNESDAY DAILY ACCOMPLISHMENT:

THURSDAY DAILY ACCOMPLISHMENT:

FRIDAY DAILY ACCOMPLISHMENT:

SATURDAY

SUNDAY

PERSONAL TO-DO LIST	WORK TO-DO LIST	PROJECT TO-DO LIST

WEEKLY ACCOMPLISHMENTS: **WEEKLY WORD COUNT:**

JOT A LINE - SKETCH A SCENE - MIND THE MUSE

"You sit down at the keyboard and you put one word after another until it's done." -Neil Gaiman

THIS WEEK'S FOCUS:

MONDAY ☐ DAILY ACCOMPLISHMENT:

___

TUESDAY ☐ DAILY ACCOMPLISHMENT:

___

WEDNESDAY ☐ DAILY ACCOMPLISHMENT:

___

THURSDAY ☐ DAILY ACCOMPLISHMENT:

___

FRIDAY ☐ DAILY ACCOMPLISHMENT:

___

SATURDAY ☐ | **SUNDAY** ☐

PERSONAL TO-DO LIST	WORK TO-DO LIST	PROJECT TO-DO LIST

WEEKLY ACCOMPLISHMENTS: **WEEKLY WORD COUNT:**

JOT A LINE - SKETCH A SCENE - MIND THE MUSE

"You have to write the book that wants to be written." -Madeleine L'Engle

THIS WEEK'S FOCUS:

MONDAY ☐ DAILY ACCOMPLISHMENT:

TUESDAY ☐ DAILY ACCOMPLISHMENT:

WEDNESDAY ☐ DAILY ACCOMPLISHMENT:

THURSDAY ☐ DAILY ACCOMPLISHMENT:

FRIDAY ☐ DAILY ACCOMPLISHMENT:

SATURDAY ☐   **SUNDAY** ☐

PERSONAL TO-DO LIST	WORK TO-DO LIST	PROJECT TO-DO LIST

WEEKLY ACCOMPLISHMENTS: **WEEKLY WORD COUNT:**

JOT A LINE - SKETCH A SCENE - MIND THE MUSE

"When writing a novel a writer should create living people; people, not characters." -Ernest Hemingway

THIS WEEK'S FOCUS:

MONDAY DAILY ACCOMPLISHMENT:
_____
_____
_____

TUESDAY DAILY ACCOMPLISHMENT:
_____
_____
_____

WEDNESDAY DAILY ACCOMPLISHMENT:
_____
_____
_____

THURSDAY DAILY ACCOMPLISHMENT:
_____
_____
_____

FRIDAY DAILY ACCOMPLISHMENT:
_____
_____
_____

SATURDAY   **SUNDAY**
_____ _____
_____ _____
_____ _____

PERSONAL TO-DO LIST	WORK TO-DO LIST	PROJECT TO-DO LIST

WEEKLY ACCOMPLISHMENTS: **WEEKLY WORD COUNT:**

JOT A LINE - SKETCH A SCENE - MIND THE MUSE

"When I say work I only mean writing. Everything else is just odd jobs." -Margaret Laurence

THIS MONTH'S FOCUS:

NOTES	SUNDAY	MONDAY	TUESDAY

GOALS / TASKS

ACCOMPLISHMENTS

NOTES

108   "My inspiration tends to come from two words.... 'what if?'" -Beth Revis

WEDNESDAY	THURSDAY	FRIDAY	SATURDAY

"You must stay drunk on writing so reality cannot destroy you." -Ray Bradbury

THIS WEEK'S FOCUS:

MONDAY DAILY ACCOMPLISHMENT:

TUESDAY DAILY ACCOMPLISHMENT:

WEDNESDAY DAILY ACCOMPLISHMENT:

THURSDAY DAILY ACCOMPLISHMENT:

FRIDAY DAILY ACCOMPLISHMENT:

SATURDAY

SUNDAY

PERSONAL TO-DO LIST	WORK TO-DO LIST	PROJECT TO-DO LIST

WEEKLY ACCOMPLISHMENTS: **WEEKLY WORD COUNT:**

JOT A LINE - SKETCH A SCENE - MIND THE MUSE

"Very few writers really know what they are doing until they've done it." -Anne Lamott

THIS WEEK'S FOCUS:

MONDAY　　DAILY ACCOMPLISHMENT:

TUESDAY　　DAILY ACCOMPLISHMENT:

WEDNESDAY　　DAILY ACCOMPLISHMENT:

THURSDAY　　DAILY ACCOMPLISHMENT:

FRIDAY　　DAILY ACCOMPLISHMENT:

SATURDAY　　　　　　　　　　　　　　**SUNDAY**

PERSONAL TO-DO LIST	WORK TO-DO LIST	PROJECT TO-DO LIST

WEEKLY ACCOMPLISHMENTS: **WEEKLY WORD COUNT:**

JOT A LINE - SKETCH A SCENE - MIND THE MUSE

"Write what disturbs you, what you fear…be willing to split open." -Natalie Goldberg

THIS WEEK'S FOCUS:

MONDAY   DAILY ACCOMPLISHMENT:

_____
_____
_____

TUESDAY   DAILY ACCOMPLISHMENT:

_____
_____
_____

WEDNESDAY   DAILY ACCOMPLISHMENT:

_____
_____
_____

THURSDAY   DAILY ACCOMPLISHMENT:

_____
_____
_____

FRIDAY   DAILY ACCOMPLISHMENT:

_____
_____
_____

SATURDAY   **SUNDAY**

_____   _____
_____   _____
_____   _____

PERSONAL TO-DO LIST	WORK TO-DO LIST	PROJECT TO-DO LIST

WEEKLY ACCOMPLISHMENTS: **WEEKLY WORD COUNT:**

JOT A LINE - SKETCH A SCENE - MIND THE MUSE

"The most beautiful things are those that madness prompts and reason writes." -Andre Gide

THIS WEEK'S FOCUS:

MONDAY DAILY ACCOMPLISHMENT:

TUESDAY DAILY ACCOMPLISHMENT:

WEDNESDAY DAILY ACCOMPLISHMENT:

THURSDAY DAILY ACCOMPLISHMENT:

FRIDAY DAILY ACCOMPLISHMENT:

SATURDAY

SUNDAY

PERSONAL TO-DO LIST	WORK TO-DO LIST	PROJECT TO-DO LIST

WEEKLY ACCOMPLISHMENTS: **WEEKLY WORD COUNT:**

JOT A LINE - SKETCH A SCENE - MIND THE MUSE

"I think all writing is a disease. You can't stop it." -William Carlos Williams

THIS WEEK'S FOCUS:

MONDAY ☐ DAILY ACCOMPLISHMENT:

TUESDAY ☐ DAILY ACCOMPLISHMENT:

WEDNESDAY ☐ DAILY ACCOMPLISHMENT:

THURSDAY ☐ DAILY ACCOMPLISHMENT:

FRIDAY ☐ DAILY ACCOMPLISHMENT:

SATURDAY ☐

SUNDAY ☐

PERSONAL TO-DO LIST	WORK TO-DO LIST	PROJECT TO-DO LIST

WEEKLY ACCOMPLISHMENTS: **WEEKLY WORD COUNT:**

JOT A LINE - SKETCH A SCENE - MIND THE MUSE

"Anyone who is going to be a writer knows enough at 15 to write several novels." -Mary Sarton

THIS MONTH'S FOCUS:

NOTES	SUNDAY	MONDAY	TUESDAY

GOALS / TASKS

ACCOMPLISHMENTS

NOTES

"A good writer is always a people watcher." -Judy Blume

WEDNESDAY	THURSDAY	FRIDAY	SATURDAY

"Description begins in the writer's imagination, but should finish in the reader's." -Stephen King

THIS WEEK'S FOCUS:

MONDAY   DAILY ACCOMPLISHMENT:
_____
_____
_____

TUESDAY   DAILY ACCOMPLISHMENT:
_____
_____
_____

WEDNESDAY   DAILY ACCOMPLISHMENT:
_____
_____
_____

THURSDAY   DAILY ACCOMPLISHMENT:
_____
_____
_____

FRIDAY   DAILY ACCOMPLISHMENT:
_____
_____
_____

SATURDAY	**SUNDAY**
_____	_____
_____	_____
_____	_____

PERSONAL TO-DO LIST	WORK TO-DO LIST	PROJECT TO-DO LIST

WEEKLY ACCOMPLISHMENTS: **WEEKLY WORD COUNT:**

JOT A LINE - SKETCH A SCENE - MIND THE MUSE

"Writing is easy. All you have to do is cross out the wrong words." -Mark Twain

| | THIS WEEK'S FOCUS: |

MONDAY ☐ DAILY ACCOMPLISHMENT:

___

TUESDAY ☐ DAILY ACCOMPLISHMENT:

___

WEDNESDAY ☐ DAILY ACCOMPLISHMENT:

___

THURSDAY ☐ DAILY ACCOMPLISHMENT:

___

FRIDAY ☐ DAILY ACCOMPLISHMENT:

___

SATURDAY ☐ | **SUNDAY** ☐

PERSONAL TO-DO LIST	WORK TO-DO LIST	PROJECT TO-DO LIST

WEEKLY ACCOMPLISHMENTS: **WEEKLY WORD COUNT:**

JOT A LINE - SKETCH A SCENE - MIND THE MUSE

"If you wait for inspiration to write, you're not a writer. You're a waiter." -Dan Poynter

THIS WEEK'S FOCUS:

MONDAY DAILY ACCOMPLISHMENT:

TUESDAY DAILY ACCOMPLISHMENT:

WEDNESDAY DAILY ACCOMPLISHMENT:

THURSDAY DAILY ACCOMPLISHMENT:

FRIDAY DAILY ACCOMPLISHMENT:

SATURDAY

SUNDAY

PERSONAL TO-DO LIST	WORK TO-DO LIST	PROJECT TO-DO LIST

WEEKLY ACCOMPLISHMENTS: **WEEKLY WORD COUNT:**

JOT A LINE - SKETCH A SCENE - MIND THE MUSE

"There is only one plot - things are not what they seem." -Jim Thompson

THIS WEEK'S FOCUS:

MONDAY ☐ DAILY ACCOMPLISHMENT:

_____
_____
_____

TUESDAY ☐ DAILY ACCOMPLISHMENT:

_____
_____
_____

WEDNESDAY ☐ DAILY ACCOMPLISHMENT:

_____
_____
_____

THURSDAY ☐ DAILY ACCOMPLISHMENT:

_____
_____
_____

FRIDAY ☐ DAILY ACCOMPLISHMENT:

_____
_____
_____

SATURDAY ☐	**SUNDAY** ☐
_____	_____
_____	_____
_____	_____
_____	_____

PERSONAL TO-DO LIST	WORK TO-DO LIST	PROJECT TO-DO LIST

WEEKLY ACCOMPLISHMENTS: **WEEKLY WORD COUNT:**

JOT A LINE - SKETCH A SCENE - MIND THE MUSE

"Just write every day of your life. Read intensely. Then see what happens." -Ray Bradbury

THIS WEEK'S FOCUS:

MONDAY ☐ DAILY ACCOMPLISHMENT:

TUESDAY ☐ DAILY ACCOMPLISHMENT:

WEDNESDAY ☐ DAILY ACCOMPLISHMENT:

THURSDAY ☐ DAILY ACCOMPLISHMENT:

FRIDAY ☐ DAILY ACCOMPLISHMENT:

SATURDAY ☐

SUNDAY ☐

PERSONAL TO-DO LIST	WORK TO-DO LIST	PROJECT TO-DO LIST

WEEKLY ACCOMPLISHMENTS: **WEEKLY WORD COUNT:**

JOT A LINE - SKETCH A SCENE - MIND THE MUSE

"They don't really need advice, they know they want to be writers, and they're gonna do it." -R.L. Stein

THIS MONTH'S FOCUS:

NOTES	SUNDAY	MONDAY	TUESDAY

GOALS / TASKS

ACCOMPLISHMENTS

NOTES

"Your intuition knows what to write, so get out of the way." -Ray Bradbury

WEDNESDAY	THURSDAY	FRIDAY	SATURDAY

"The desire to write grows with writing." -Erasmus

THIS WEEK'S FOCUS:

MONDAY ☐ DAILY ACCOMPLISHMENT:

_____
_____
_____

TUESDAY ☐ DAILY ACCOMPLISHMENT:

_____
_____
_____

WEDNESDAY ☐ DAILY ACCOMPLISHMENT:

_____
_____
_____

THURSDAY ☐ DAILY ACCOMPLISHMENT:

_____
_____
_____

FRIDAY ☐ DAILY ACCOMPLISHMENT:

_____
_____
_____

SATURDAY ☐ | **SUNDAY** ☐

_____ | _____
_____ | _____
_____ | _____

PERSONAL TO-DO LIST	WORK TO-DO LIST	PROJECT TO-DO LIST

WEEKLY ACCOMPLISHMENTS: **WEEKLY WORD COUNT:**

JOT A LINE - SKETCH A SCENE - MIND THE MUSE

"You need a certain amount of nerve to be a writer." -Margaret Atwood

THIS WEEK'S FOCUS:

MONDAY DAILY ACCOMPLISHMENT:

TUESDAY DAILY ACCOMPLISHMENT:

WEDNESDAY DAILY ACCOMPLISHMENT:

THURSDAY DAILY ACCOMPLISHMENT:

FRIDAY DAILY ACCOMPLISHMENT:

SATURDAY **SUNDAY**

PERSONAL TO-DO LIST	WORK TO-DO LIST	PROJECT TO-DO LIST

WEEKLY ACCOMPLISHMENTS: **WEEKLY WORD COUNT:**

___

JOT A LINE - SKETCH A SCENE - MIND THE MUSE

"Better to write for yourself and have no public than to write for the public and have no self." -Cyril Connolly

THIS WEEK'S FOCUS:

MONDAY   DAILY ACCOMPLISHMENT:
_____
_____
_____

TUESDAY   DAILY ACCOMPLISHMENT:
_____
_____
_____

WEDNESDAY   DAILY ACCOMPLISHMENT:
_____
_____
_____

THURSDAY   DAILY ACCOMPLISHMENT:
_____
_____
_____

FRIDAY   DAILY ACCOMPLISHMENT:
_____
_____
_____

SATURDAY
_____
_____
_____

SUNDAY
_____
_____
_____

PERSONAL TO-DO LIST	WORK TO-DO LIST	PROJECT TO-DO LIST

WEEKLY ACCOMPLISHMENTS: **WEEKLY WORD COUNT:**

JOT A LINE - SKETCH A SCENE - MIND THE MUSE

"All stories have to at least try to explain some small portion of the meaning of life." -Gene Weingarten

THIS WEEK'S FOCUS:

MONDAY DAILY ACCOMPLISHMENT:

TUESDAY DAILY ACCOMPLISHMENT:

WEDNESDAY DAILY ACCOMPLISHMENT:

THURSDAY DAILY ACCOMPLISHMENT:

FRIDAY DAILY ACCOMPLISHMENT:

SATURDAY   **SUNDAY**

PERSONAL TO-DO LIST	WORK TO-DO LIST	PROJECT TO-DO LIST

WEEKLY ACCOMPLISHMENTS: **WEEKLY WORD COUNT:**

JOT A LINE - SKETCH A SCENE - MIND THE MUSE

"You will either write or you will not - and the only way to find out whether you will or not is to try." -Jim Tully

THIS WEEK'S FOCUS:

MONDAY DAILY ACCOMPLISHMENT:

TUESDAY DAILY ACCOMPLISHMENT:

WEDNESDAY DAILY ACCOMPLISHMENT:

THURSDAY DAILY ACCOMPLISHMENT:

FRIDAY DAILY ACCOMPLISHMENT:

SATURDAY

SUNDAY

PERSONAL TO-DO LIST	WORK TO-DO LIST	PROJECT TO-DO LIST

WEEKLY ACCOMPLISHMENTS: **WEEKLY WORD COUNT:**

___

JOT A LINE - SKETCH A SCENE - MIND THE MUSE

"When your story is ready for rewrite, cut it to the bone." -Stephen King

THIS MONTH'S FOCUS:

NOTES	SUNDAY	MONDAY	TUESDAY

GOALS / TASKS

ACCOMPLISHMENTS

NOTES

"A writer is working when he's staring out the window." -Burton Rascoe

WEDNESDAY	THURSDAY	FRIDAY	SATURDAY

"Don't be paralyzed by the idea that you're writing a book; just write." -Isabelle Allende

THIS WEEK'S FOCUS:

MONDAY DAILY ACCOMPLISHMENT:

_____
_____
_____

TUESDAY DAILY ACCOMPLISHMENT:

_____
_____
_____

WEDNESDAY DAILY ACCOMPLISHMENT:

_____
_____
_____

THURSDAY DAILY ACCOMPLISHMENT:

_____
_____
_____

FRIDAY DAILY ACCOMPLISHMENT:

_____
_____
_____

SATURDAY　　　　　　　　　　　　　**SUNDAY**

_____　　_____
_____　　_____
_____　　_____

PERSONAL TO-DO LIST	WORK TO-DO LIST	PROJECT TO-DO LIST

WEEKLY ACCOMPLISHMENTS: **WEEKLY WORD COUNT:**

JOT A LINE - SKETCH A SCENE - MIND THE MUSE

"If I waited till I felt like writing, I'd never write at all." -Anne Tyler

THIS WEEK'S FOCUS:

MONDAY   DAILY ACCOMPLISHMENT:

TUESDAY   DAILY ACCOMPLISHMENT:

WEDNESDAY   DAILY ACCOMPLISHMENT:

THURSDAY   DAILY ACCOMPLISHMENT:

FRIDAY   DAILY ACCOMPLISHMENT:

SATURDAY

SUNDAY

PERSONAL TO-DO LIST	WORK TO-DO LIST	PROJECT TO-DO LIST

WEEKLY ACCOMPLISHMENTS: **WEEKLY WORD COUNT:**

_____
_____
_____
_____
_____
_____
_____
_____

JOT A LINE - SKETCH A SCENE - MIND THE MUSE

"Don't be a writer. Be writing." -William Faulkner

THIS WEEK'S FOCUS:

MONDAY DAILY ACCOMPLISHMENT:

_____
_____
_____

TUESDAY DAILY ACCOMPLISHMENT:

_____
_____
_____

WEDNESDAY DAILY ACCOMPLISHMENT:

_____
_____
_____

THURSDAY DAILY ACCOMPLISHMENT:

_____
_____
_____

FRIDAY DAILY ACCOMPLISHMENT:

_____
_____
_____

SATURDAY	**SUNDAY**
_____	_____
_____	_____
_____	_____

PERSONAL TO-DO LIST	WORK TO-DO LIST	PROJECT TO-DO LIST

WEEKLY ACCOMPLISHMENTS: **WEEKLY WORD COUNT:**

JOT A LINE - SKETCH A SCENE - MIND THE MUSE

"Plot is people. Human emotions and desires founded on the realities of life..." -Lee Brackett

THIS WEEK'S FOCUS:

MONDAY DAILY ACCOMPLISHMENT:

TUESDAY DAILY ACCOMPLISHMENT:

WEDNESDAY DAILY ACCOMPLISHMENT:

THURSDAY DAILY ACCOMPLISHMENT:

FRIDAY DAILY ACCOMPLISHMENT:

SATURDAY

SUNDAY

PERSONAL TO-DO LIST	WORK TO-DO LIST	PROJECT TO-DO LIST

WEEKLY ACCOMPLISHMENTS: **WEEKLY WORD COUNT:**

JOT A LINE - SKETCH A SCENE - MIND THE MUSE

"Style means the right word. The rest matters little." -Jules Renard

THIS WEEK'S FOCUS:

MONDAY   DAILY ACCOMPLISHMENT:

TUESDAY   DAILY ACCOMPLISHMENT:

WEDNESDAY   DAILY ACCOMPLISHMENT:

THURSDAY   DAILY ACCOMPLISHMENT:

FRIDAY   DAILY ACCOMPLISHMENT:

SATURDAY   **SUNDAY**

PERSONAL TO-DO LIST	WORK TO-DO LIST	PROJECT TO-DO LIST

WEEKLY ACCOMPLISHMENTS: **WEEKLY WORD COUNT:**

JOT A LINE - SKETCH A SCENE - MIND THE MUSE

"There are no laws for the novel. There never have been, nor can there ever be." -Doris Lessing

THIS MONTH'S FOCUS:

NOTES	SUNDAY	MONDAY	TUESDAY

GOALS / TASKS

ACCOMPLISHMENTS

NOTES

"Write hard and clear about what hurts." -Ernest Hemingway

WEDNESDAY	THURSDAY	FRIDAY	SATURDAY

"If it sounds like writing, I rewrite it." -Elmore Leonard

THIS WEEK'S FOCUS:

MONDAY DAILY ACCOMPLISHMENT:

TUESDAY DAILY ACCOMPLISHMENT:

WEDNESDAY DAILY ACCOMPLISHMENT:

THURSDAY DAILY ACCOMPLISHMENT:

FRIDAY DAILY ACCOMPLISHMENT:

SATURDAY

SUNDAY

PERSONAL TO-DO LIST	WORK TO-DO LIST	PROJECT TO-DO LIST

WEEKLY ACCOMPLISHMENTS: **WEEKLY WORD COUNT:**

JOT A LINE - SKETCH A SCENE - MIND THE MUSE

"When we write, we start in the middle and fight our way out." -Vickie Karp

THIS WEEK'S FOCUS:

MONDAY DAILY ACCOMPLISHMENT:

TUESDAY DAILY ACCOMPLISHMENT:

WEDNESDAY DAILY ACCOMPLISHMENT:

THURSDAY DAILY ACCOMPLISHMENT:

FRIDAY DAILY ACCOMPLISHMENT:

SATURDAY

SUNDAY

PERSONAL TO-DO LIST	WORK TO-DO LIST	PROJECT TO-DO LIST

WEEKLY ACCOMPLISHMENTS: **WEEKLY WORD COUNT:**

JOT A LINE - SKETCH A SCENE - MIND THE MUSE

"Keep scribbling! Something will happen." -Frank McCourt

THIS WEEK'S FOCUS:

MONDAY DAILY ACCOMPLISHMENT:

_____
_____
_____

TUESDAY DAILY ACCOMPLISHMENT:

_____
_____
_____

WEDNESDAY DAILY ACCOMPLISHMENT:

_____
_____
_____

THURSDAY DAILY ACCOMPLISHMENT:

_____
_____
_____

FRIDAY DAILY ACCOMPLISHMENT:

_____
_____
_____

SATURDAY	**SUNDAY**
_____	_____
_____	_____
_____	_____

PERSONAL TO-DO LIST	WORK TO-DO LIST	PROJECT TO-DO LIST

WEEKLY ACCOMPLISHMENTS: **WEEKLY WORD COUNT:**

JOT A LINE - SKETCH A SCENE - MIND THE MUSE

"Write. Rewrite. When not writing or rewriting, read. I know of no shortcuts." -Larry L. King

THIS WEEK'S FOCUS:

MONDAY DAILY ACCOMPLISHMENT:

TUESDAY DAILY ACCOMPLISHMENT:

WEDNESDAY DAILY ACCOMPLISHMENT:

THURSDAY DAILY ACCOMPLISHMENT:

FRIDAY DAILY ACCOMPLISHMENT:

SATURDAY

SUNDAY

PERSONAL TO-DO LIST	WORK TO-DO LIST	PROJECT TO-DO LIST

WEEKLY ACCOMPLISHMENTS: **WEEKLY WORD COUNT:**

JOT A LINE - SKETCH A SCENE - MIND THE MUSE

"We are all apprentices in a craft where no one ever becomes a master." -Ernest Hemingway

THIS WEEK'S FOCUS:

MONDAY ☐ DAILY ACCOMPLISHMENT:

_____
_____
_____

TUESDAY ☐ DAILY ACCOMPLISHMENT:

_____
_____
_____

WEDNESDAY ☐ DAILY ACCOMPLISHMENT:

_____
_____
_____

THURSDAY ☐ DAILY ACCOMPLISHMENT:

_____
_____
_____

FRIDAY ☐ DAILY ACCOMPLISHMENT:

_____
_____
_____

SATURDAY ☐	**SUNDAY** ☐
_____	_____
_____	_____
_____	_____

PERSONAL TO-DO LIST	WORK TO-DO LIST	PROJECT TO-DO LIST

WEEKLY ACCOMPLISHMENTS: **WEEKLY WORD COUNT:**

JOT A LINE - SKETCH A SCENE - MIND THE MUSE

"Not a wasted word. This has been a main point to my literary thinking all my life." -Hunter S. Thompson

"YOU ARE NEVER TOO OLD TO SET ANOTHER GOAL OR TO DREAM A NEW DREAM."

—C.S. LEWIS, AUTHOR

WELCOME TO YOUR BRAINSTORMING & RESOURCES CENTER

KEEP DREAMING. KEEP LEARNING.

STORY IDEAS

IDEA TITLE: **IDEA SUMMARY:**

GENRE: _____
SETTING: _____

CHARACTERS: _____

IDEA TITLE: **IDEA SUMMARY:**

GENRE: _____
SETTING: _____

CHARACTERS: _____

IDEA TITLE: **IDEA SUMMARY:**

GENRE: _____
SETTING: _____

CHARACTERS: _____

IDEA TITLE: **IDEA SUMMARY:**

GENRE: _____
SETTING: _____

CHARACTERS: _____

IDEA TITLE: **IDEA SUMMARY:**

GENRE: _____
SETTING: _____

CHARACTERS: _____

TO-BE-READ LIST

READ?	BOOK TITLE	AUTHOR	GENRE

SKETCH SPACE FOR YOU, MY FRIEND!

SKETCH SPACE FOR YOU, MY FRIEND!

SKETCH SPACE FOR YOU, MY FRIEND!

SKETCH SPACE FOR YOU, MY FRIEND!

" OPTIMISM IS THE FAITH THAT LEADS TO ACHIEVEMENT. NOTHING CAN BE DONE WITHOUT HOPE AND CONFIDENCE."

-HELEN KELLER, AUTHOR AND POLITICAL ACTIVIST

WELCOME TO YOUR YEARLY ACHIEVEMENTS TRACKER

IT'S PARTY TIME. LET'S CELEBRATE!

CELEBRATING ACHIEVEMENTS

DATE	ACHIEVEMENT	REWARD

CELEBRATING ACHIEVEMENTS

DATE	ACHIEVEMENT	REWARD

| DATE | ACHIEVEMENT | REWARD |

DID YOU HAVE AN AMAZING YEAR?

THE NOVEL PLANNER

A DAILY PLANNER FOR AUTHORS

I HOPE YOU'VE ENJOYED USING THE NOVEL PLANNER TO ORGANIZE YOUR DAY.

IF YOU HAVE ANY SUGGESTIONS FOR THE PLANNER'S IMPROVEMENT OR WOULD LIKE TO GET IN TOUCH, DON'T HESITATE TO SAY HELLO!

- FIND ME ON TWITTER, INSTAGRAM, AND PINTEREST - @SHESNOVEL -
- FACEBOOK.COM/SHESNOVEL -
- PLUS.GOOGLE.COM/+SHESNOVEL -
- SHESNOVEL.COM -

THANK YOU AND DON'T FORGET TO STAY AMAZING!

Made in the USA
Lexington, KY
28 May 2016